MICAH'S STORY

REDEFINING MS

www.selfpublishn30days.com

Published by Self Publish -N- 30 Days

Printed in the United States of America

ISBN: 978-1720652748

1. Inspiration 2. Self Help

Micah Love: E3twenty

Micah's Story

Disclaimer/Warning:

This book is intended for lecture and entertainment purposes only. The author or publisher does not guarantee that anyone following these steps will be successful in overcoming challenges. The author and publisher shall have neither liability responsibility to anyone with respect to any loss or damage cause, or alleged to be caused, directly or indirectly by the information contained in this book. The MS Society has not supported and is not a sponsor of this book. This was written independent of the National MS Society.

IN MEMORY OF

DEBRAH ALFORD
VALERIE HARRIS-POLE
RODRICK "BIG ROD" JACQUET

DEDICATION

I dedicate this book to the foundation of my life, my family.
My hand delivered wife from God, Candice
My two sons, Luke & Lance
My parents, Robert & Lynn Love
My sister, Joy Love
My niece/daughter, Alaina Hawkins

ACKNOWLEDGEMENTS

I would like to acknowledge all of the individuals who have had a hand in writing the script of Micah's Story. Time will never let me forget what you all have done for me. I just want to say, "Thank you."

Tim Clipson @ the entire Life Staff

Pastor Alan Lamar Patterson

Ian & Frene Chestnut

Sick wit-it Records Crew

Corinth Church Family

All my cousins & relatives (The MS warriors in the family)

Kappa Alpha Psi Mu Sigma Chapter Fall 97'

The Houston Chapter of the MS Society

TJ & Shamika Harris

Bruce West

Calvin Taylor

Phill & Zeora Jackson

Darren M. Palmer

Dr. William Lyndsey

Dr. Angel Perez

CONTENTS

INTRODUCTION

Stor•y. /stórē/

Noun:

1. An account of imagery or real people and events told for entertainment

2. An account of past events in someone's life or in the evolution of something

Webster's description of a story is a pretty accurate representation of what you will read in *Micah's Story - Redefining MS*.

Imagery has been painted in the minds of many people about what an MS patient should look like, what that patient should believe and how they should act. *Micah's Story* presents imagery of a real person with this real disease.

There are countless stories that can be told because of my experiences with multiple sclerosis. This book will show my evolution and how I am trying to redefine MS in my own way.

While you read this, please do me a favor: use this book to increase your awareness of MS, understand MS patients and, most of all, be entertained.

CHAPTER ONE

Bar-B-Que or Mildew

It was a sunny, chilly Saturday morning, about twelve miles outside of a pleasant town called Fayetteville, Texas. I was one of 13,000 amateur cyclists headed to Austin on a bike! The small, but flamboyant team I co-founded and named 'Ridin' Dirty' was moving at a great pace. I was about six bikes behind our lead rider. Around this time, as I'd done so often, I did a full body check.

How does my head feel? Ok, no headache ✔.

Shoulders? A little tight, so roll neck, stretch out and drop my shoulders a little. Ok ✔.

Back? A little over-extended, so sit up a little. Ok ✔.

Wiggle my fingers and stretch my wrists... Ok ✔.

Ok now wiggle my toes. Wait...well that feels strange.

Wiggle them again...still feels strange.

Well, umm, I really can't feel my toes.

Ok, well let's work our way up.

Can I feel my feet? No, not really. Ok, let's do one leg at a time.

Can I feel my right leg? Ok. How about the left one? Nope, that's gone.

So, from the knee down, through the entire foot...nothing.

This is not good, but I know it could be worse. I try to make some adjustments while riding, but I quickly realize that there are really no adjustments for this kind of thing. The good thing is, I knew I could still pedal, but when it was time to unclip and get off the bike, I might have a slight problem.

I continued to ride along with the team. They felt me slow down a bit but I told them to go ahead; I didn't want to hold them up. They gracefully denied me solitude and slowed down to ride at my pace. It was great for moral support but bad for the team.

Other riders that I had recently passed were passing me now. All of them were asking, "Hey Micah, are you ok?" The question was brought on by my slow pace but I'm sure they could see the anguish on my face. Couple that with the 'I Ride Because I Have MS' jersey I was wearing and I'm sure their concern was heightened.

There was a decision to make. I sometimes considered it an excuse, not a decision, but I had to decide: do I want to stop and get assistance or do I want to power through? After training for several months and joined by close friends, who either rode along or supported financially, I really did not want to let this lack of feeling in my leg and feet stop me.

Riding in the BP MS 150 is not an easy task for a healthy, amateur rider, let alone someone with MS. The ride from Houston to Austin, Texas is the largest bike ride of its kind in North America. It aims to raise funds for research and support the work towards a cure for Multiple Sclerosis. Since its inception in 1983, it has grown to attract more than 13,000 riders per year and has raised over $250 million.

I am always down to help a worthy cause, but, for this one, I was double-down.

All of these thoughts brought me back to my 'why'. As I did my body check, the crank on my bike was still spinning, powered by one leg that still had some feeling in it. This ride was tough and I'd asked myself why all day. Whether you were riding for kicks, riding for a loved one or just riding because you lost a bet…anyone would ask why.

WHAT WAS MY WHY AS A PERSON WITH MS?

At the very least, I knew I had to help myself. I'd heard this saying from my sister: 'Are you going to Bar-B-Que or mildew?' (thanks Joy!). It means are you going to act or not. Well, I like Bar-B-Que, so there it was. I was riding and there was really no question about the why.

I must admit that during this ride, I was thinking a little selfishly. In my mind all 13,000 riders were riding just for me. They were riding for a cure for MICAH LOVE.

It was like I was the only person in the world with this disease. Because of that, I tried to thank as many people as possible before, during and after the ride. My life with MS has many facets and I want to explain them to you from a mindset of a person with the disease and how ok it all is.

THIS IS MICAH'S STORY

Let's take it back to who I was right before I was diagnosed with MS.

In the fall of 1998, I was a junior at Stephen F. Austin State University, majoring in International Business. I was an active, no, a very active student. I was a part of at least six different clubs, three organizations and a member of the one and only fraternity, Kappa Alpha Psi... Shout out to my Nupes! I held the best job on campus and had two off-campus jobs in the city. I was also an orientation leader in the summers and an ambassador for the university during the school year. To say the least, I did a lot. I'd even started an alumni charter chapter.

I was the student who had lunch with the mayor of Nacogdoches and dinner with university families in the same day. My life as a collegiate was grand. My stock was on the rise. As I look back on my college days, it was the social vacation of my life. I was in a nice groove. I knew a ton of people and a ton of people knew me. Life was good and getting better.

I'm sure you have heard the statement 'If you fail to plan, then you plan to fail'.

Up until that point, I had been winging it and was blessed with the direction my life was going. However, as a smart, young college person, I decided to make a plan. I decided that when I graduated in the spring of 2000, I would enter the Air Force Academy, become an officer and then eventually transition into being a commercial airline pilot. Really!

I knew no cooler job: you got to travel, see the world, meet many different people and be in and out of countries, jet-setting. You were able to operate the most modern aircraft technology. It would be like operating the longest Cadillac ever made. I was willing to be responsible for all the lives in my hands. In addition to all of that, you got to skip the line at all the airports and wear THE uniform, even though I thought the hat would look goofy on me. And I would be getting paid!

Now that was the dream job for Micah Love.

Can you hear it? "This is your pilot Micah Love, just sit back and relax," in my Barry White voice.

Can't you just imagine it? Yeah, me too!

Ok, so back to being a great college student. It was time to celebrate…Where was the party? After all, I had figured it out my plan. The fall semester rolled by and it was time to go home for Christmas. It was the best time of the year to me as a college student. The year was halfway finished and I got to go home to Christmas family gatherings, food and parties. Speaking of parties, a few frat brothers and I decided to drive to Houston for a night to partake in the annual college party at The Downtown Tavern in Houston! This college party was everything you'd imagine it to be. They were special in Houston around that time of the year. You would have college students from all over that were back home and catching up with old friends from high school.

Plus, you would also be there with your new friends from college. There was a double whammy of having all your friends in one place partying! Trust me, they were wonderful times.

After the party, my frat brothers and I slept at my parents' home and, the next day, we drove the two hours back to S.F.A. to see everybody's friend, Big Rod (Play In Heaven), graduate.

It was a rainy, chilly winter day in Texas and I was driving my roommate's car for him because he had partied a little too hard the night before. We were almost back at school when all the red break lights in front of us flashed suddenly. Everyone jumped on their brakes, even though I was the only one driving. But these were college kids' tires and they were as bald as boloney.

Well, you guessed it, we slid and hit the car in front of us, an Armed Forces service car. It really was a minor finder bender. No one was hurt and we only had a bumper scratch and a broken headlight. My bad (sorry again J. Green)!

All was well, though. We still went to the graduation and saw our guy graduate. It was still a great day for everybody. After that, we all returned to our respective cities to continue the holiday break.

The following week, when I was back in Houston I decided to play a game of basketball. It was one of my loves and a favorite hobby for me and all the fellas from way back. It was our getaway and excuse to get together. It was a good basketball session that day… messed around and got a triple-double!

Afterwards, I went home but something just didn't feel right. It was like I'd pulled something, like a muscle on my right-side oblique. I took a hot shower to ease the pain. That made it worse. The pain spread from my right midsection to my right upper thigh.

So there I was, sitting in my parents' home, trying to figure out what was wrong. Maybe something was strained? But no, this feeling was a little too strange. Then I remembered I'd had the car accident a week before. Ah that's it, I may have a pinched nerve during the accident! Yeah, that is it, it's from the accident. Ok, so Dr. Love had diagnosed himself. It was a pinched nerve.

My long-time neighbor Byron owned a few physical therapy clinics in Houston. I saw him in his driveway and told him what was wrong. He said, "I'm not sure that's a pinched nerve. It's Christmas and all of my clinics are closed for the holidays, but let me call one of my doctors to see if he will take a look at you." Ok great! I was ready to get any kind of help at that point. It was an odd feeling. Yes, there was pain, but there was also this weird discomfort.

After two days passed, Byron got a doctor to open his clinic for me. I saw him right away. He did movement and pressure point tests and I passed them all. There was no nerve damage and no pulled muscles. Uuummm, so what's the problem? The doctor suggested I see a neurologist. Ok, that was different. I now had a mission.

The next day, which was the 29th of December 1998, I was able to get into Dr. Chris Loar's office, a licensed MD who specialized in neurology. He was a great doctor. My mom went with me so we could find out what was going on. We filled out all the new patient paperwork and then went into a patient room.

In walked Dr. Loar, who was about six feet tall. He was a slim, clean-cut, bearded white man with brown hair. He had a few freckles on his nose and a gentle smile with trusting eyes. He looked like he could be Mr. Rogers' brother. He also had a calm demeanor and was easy-going and very likable.

He looked at my chart and we talked for a while about my situation. He looked a little puzzled. He said, "Ok, stand up and follow me." He commenced to perform a series of tests on me; tests that were similar to field sobriety tests. You know, the hold your head back, finger to nose type deal; the follow my finger with your eyes business. I was getting a kick out of it because I was passing all of them with no problem. Then I did the all-time famous heel to toe test. I was low-key thinking that he was testing me for drugs or something. He said, "Put your heel to your toe and walk across this room from one corner to the opposite, diagonal corner."

Ok, this was a piece of cake because my friends and I had practiced this at school so we wouldn't end up spending a good party night in the clink. I concentrated super hard and made sure I was connecting heel to toe. Step by step, I was making it happen. I was thinking that this was easy, no sweat. I finally reached the corner, looked up, and said, "Ok done."

My mom and Dr. Loar looked confused. I wondered what was wrong. Then I examined the room and realized I was in the corner to my immediate right, not diagonally across. Wait, what just happened? So now I was looking confused.

He had me sit down and take off my shoes and socks. He broke out the ol' reflex test with the hammer. He focused on my left side ankle, knee, wrist and elbow. All reflexes looked normal. Then he went to my right elbow and wrist, which both checked out great. Then he focused on my right knee and ankle. Little to nothing happened.

He shook his head and tried it again.

The same…no reflexes. He looked in a drawer next to his computer and pulled out a safety pin. He opened it up and told me to let him know if I could feel the small point of the pin.

On my left ankle yes; on my right, not really.

On my left calf yes; on my right not really.

On my left hip, yes; on my right hip, not really.

On my left rib cage, yes; on my right rib cage, not really.

The doctor then said, "Ok," and left the room.

I was just wondering what in the world was going on when he came back in the room. He told me that all the tests I took were to see if I had the symptoms of MS. He still wasn't sure and said he would recommend more tests. I was like, "Great let's do it!"

Little did I know what having MS would actually mean. I had no idea what MS was. He told me that the next test would be an MRI of my brain and spine. That seemed so strange and extreme. Why did I need all of that?

After all, it was just a pinched nerve as per Dr. Love! So, now we are off to get the orders from the nurse and go to the MRI center.

We went to the center, which was in a strip mall. It was super cold and the building wasn't exactly welcoming. MRI machines are big, narrow tubes, just large enough to fit a human body.

I was not normally afraid of confined spaces, but it was ridiculous how small the space was. They offered me a Valium. I declined, but once I got in the machine, I had them pull me out to give me some drugs for this first episode.

Plus, I was going to be in there for an hour! Yes, give me the drugs please! Needless to say, that nap in the MRI machine and in the car ride home and then at home was the best rest I had had in days.

On December 30th, we were back into Dr. Loar's office looking and examining the recently taken MRI scan. He put on his little Walmart glasses, did the medical squint and scratched his beard a bit. He sat back in his seat with a pause and a long sigh. He pointed to the MRI film on the wall and said, "Well, all these signs are positive. You failed the motor skills test and here on the MRI there are sclerotic lesions (spots) on your brain and your spine."

There was the silence of ignorance from me. I still did not know what MS was.

Then he broke the silence and said, "We have one more test!"

I said, "Ok, great. But wait, do I need to pass or fail this one?"

He laughed and said, "Fail. This one you need to fail."

I said, "Hey, I can do that, no problem."

He said the last and final tell-all test would be a spinal tap.

A lumbar puncture, also known as a spinal tap, is a medical procedure in which a needle is inserted into the spinal canal to collect cerebrospinal fluid for diagnostic testing.

At that time, I had no clue what that was either. I was just informed to be at the hospital a 7:00 am on January 1, 1999. It was an outpatient visit but it would last at least eight hours, and I would have to remain in the hospital for the entire time. That is a long time for just a test, right? He told me to rest and that he would see me in the morning.

Morning came extremely fast. I was up at 5:30 in the morning getting prepared mentally for… what? I didn't know at all.

All I knew was, I would get a spinal tap in a few hours.

I did the morning ritual – brushed teeth, showered, ate, got dressed and headed out. The long, quiet ride to the hospital wasn't settling and it seemed to go by quicker than normal.

We arrived at the hospital and went to the outpatient center. I gave them my name and ID and they gave me this beautiful hospital-issued gown with my hind parts out and told me to get naked and put it on. They badged me up and sent me on my way.

I did all that was required quickly — you would have too if you had seen how the nurse had her beard trimmed up! A half-hour passed by and I was sitting on the side of the hospital bed.

The doctor walked in with morning greetings and a basket full of huge empty test tubes, eight to be exact. He started to explain what we were getting ready to do. He told me to lay on my left side. Once on the left side, I would curl up in the fetus position and hold on to the railings of the bed.

The reason for the fetus position was because he needed all the space he could get between the vertebrae in my spine to extract fluids.

Wait a minute! What did he say?!? He said, "Yes, this is the spinal tap."

I told him all of this was not in his pamphlet in the waiting room. He laughed, but I didn't. Then, in walked Mrs. T, the bearded nurse, to have me sign waiver papers. She mentioned the possibility of paralysis from the procedure and so forth, and to sign here by the X.

That's when this got real to me! If I had to go through all of this to make sure I had MS, then this MS stuff must be serious.

At that point, I put on my big boy pants mentally and said, "Let's get it!" I lay on my left side and balled up in the fetus position and held on for dear life or dear non-paralysis. He warned me of the prick or sharp feeling, but told me, "Please do not jump!"

Well, that whole mind over matter thing works if you don't mind to matter, especially if you are doing what you are told to prevent further damage. He stabbed me. The needle felt like it was the size of a #2 pencil. It went into my back to extract spinal fluids out of my central nervous system. He collected spinal fluid in all eight test tubes. This fluid, once tested, would show the correct proteins to get a clear diagnosis of MS. I could feel every exchange of every test tube as he collected the fluid.

He completed the process. I hadn't moved and all his tubes were full so I figured it was a successful extraction. I was not paralyzed so I was good to go. Well, yes and no.

Remember the eight hours? I still had to stay in the hospital. The reason for the eight-hour stay was because my central nervous system has been depleted of spinal fluid. The fluid's job is to pad the spine and brain and any excessive movement could cause damage. At the very least, I would have a severe headache, which I had anyway because I realized I still had to stay. The bright side was that hospitals have great drugs and they were able to make me comfortable.

I proceeded to recover in the hospital for the next seven hours. I would also get my results that day. After hanging in the hospital bed for the full seven hours, the doctor walked in, with a regretful look and what looked like tears in his eyes. He informed me that he was sorry to tell me, but my tests showed that I had the proteins which confirmed a positive MS diagnosis.

The first thing I said was, "Well, I passed the test!"

The Dr. chuckled and said, "Well, that's a good way of looking at it."

And this was the start of Micah's Story.

CHAPTER TWO

What Is This Dis-Ease?

Pastor A. Louis Patterson Jr. once explained that if you broke down the word 'disease' it would read 'dis-ease'. In the grand scheme of things, that makes a ton of sense. In disease, the 'dis' denotes a separation or a parting from; 'ease' is a freedom from difficulty or hardship or effort.

If you put all of it together, it means parting from being free of difficulty. To say it even simpler, it ain't an easy time! Ok, that last part was the Micah version of disease. But it still holds true and I'm going to tell you about the Dis-Ease of Multiple Sclerosis in good ol' Micah Love fashion.

You ready? Here we go.

So you have your central nervous system (CNS), which consists of your brain and your spinal cord that branches to the millions of finite nerves in your body. From the very top of your head down to your pinky toe, you have a nerve response or connection. It is all over your body and all means all! Ok, now you know where it is (everywhere), let me tell you what it does.

The CNS controls your body's reflexes, large and small. It also controls your flight or fight response. Basically, it controls all that you do in stressful situations.

Let's circle back to the reflexes and examine how the CNS is built. There is the center of the spine or your spinal cord and, of course, there are nerves. As you go inside the nerves, you have more nerves and neurons. Neurons connect with one another to send and receive messages in the brain and spinal cord. Many neurons working together are responsible for every decision made, every emotion or sensation felt and every action taken.

The complexity of the central nervous system is amazing: there are approximately 100 billion neurons in the brain and spinal cord combined. As many as 10,000 different subtypes of neurons have been identified, each specialized to send and receive certain types of information.

Each neuron is made up of a cell body, which houses the nucleus. Axons and dendrites form extensions from the cell body. This is how the brain sends signals to the rest of your body. The signal going back and forth smoothly is important.

A major part of the CNS that pertains to MS is the thin coating (insulation) called myelin. It is like the passing signal and lubricant for each nerve. When all of that is in good condition, all functions well. To give you a visual, think of it like the insulation over an electrical wire or the paper around a straw. If you damage either one, the wire and straw are exposed.

WHY IS THIS IMPORTANT TO MS?

You must follow this part: MS is an autoimmune dis-ease, which is caused by the reaction of antibodies to substances occurring naturally in the body. When you have it, your own body begins attacking itself. The body, once working correctly, is made to fight off the bad things that enter it. It has little soldier cells that fight day and night to prevent you from getting sick.

However, with an autoimmune dis-ease like MS, your soldier T-cells go rouge and fight against you. Their favorite place to battle is on the myelin.

This coating/lubrication is attacked and chipped away until the nerves are exposed. But then a good thing happens: the body has a reaction to it and applies scar tissue (lesions) to protect the nerves. Actually, that is a good and bad thing. It's good because it's protecting the nerves, but bad because that band-aid (lesion) is not the original lubrication and it's not smooth.

When the signals are sent, they are now slow and the reactions are also slow or non-existent. It's like a street: the road is working well until it's damaged with a pothole. The pothole is huge and slows or stops traffic. The traffic can't flow as it should, so the city emergency crew rolls up and patches it, but they don't smooth out the repair to make it flush with the rest of the road.

So, traffic may continue to be slowed or stopped.

But you know what? The pothole is still fixed and, in some cases, the city may eventually rebuild the road, bringing things back to normal. Does the same thing happen with myelin? The answer is maybe both.

Some say you cannot rejuvenate myelin and some say you can over time. I'm not sure so I can't make a medical claim one way or the other.

Even though I don't know for sure, I still ask myself why wouldn't the central nervous system be able to repair itself after an injury?

Many organs and tissues in the body can recover after injury without intervention. Unfortunately, some cells of the central nervous system are so specialized that they cannot divide and create new cells.

As a result, recovery from a brain or spinal cord injury is much more difficult. Also, if nerve exposure is too severe, the nerve may die and then the sense or reflex for which it is responsible, would be permanently impaired.

To understand fully, we must look at the CNS and all that it controls. It is essentially the electrical system of your body. For those car enthusiasts out there, it is the wiring harness for your body. The brain is the center of our thoughts, the interpreter of our external environment and the origin of control over body movement.

Like a central computer, it interprets information from our eyes (sight), ears (sound), nose (smell), tongue (taste), and skin (touch), as well as from internal organs such as the stomach.

The CNS covers so much in your body and, because of that, the effects of MS seem endless.

MS SYMPTOMS:

- The most common early symptoms include:
- Tingling
- Numbness
- Loss of balance
- Weakness in one or more limbs
- Blurred or double vision
- Less-common warning signs may be:
- Slurred speech
- Suddenly not being able to move part of your body or paralysis
- Lack of coordination
- Problems with thinking and processing information

- Pain in the eye
- Blurred vision
- Graying of vision
- Blindness in one eye
- Fatigue
- Balance and coordination problems
- Spasticity
- Bladder Dysfunction
- Constipation
- Vertigo
- Sexual dysfunction
- Depression
- Cognitive dysfunction
- Anxiety
- Emotional changes

These are just a few. Like I said, the CNS controls everything, voluntary and involuntary. This makes MS a truly unpredictable dis-ease.

CHAPTER THREE

When It All Falls Down!

When it all hits the fan for an MS patient, the effects may be totally different from a normal person. How external factors impact MS patients are varied and unpredictable. In the chapter before, I explained to you what MS the dis-ease is Now. I want to tell you firsthand what happens when it all falls down.

First, let me say that I have had several exacerbations in the past twenty years; most of them were completely different. The first was when I was first diagnosed. I had the MS numbness from my lower right chest down to the bottom of my foot on the right side only. This lasted for about two weeks.

Thinking back, it was not that severe as others. Really, it was very minor. That time, I was treated with a high dose of steroids, one of the treatments available to counter MS exacerbations.

I want to try to explain what MS numbness feels like. When the average person thinks of numbness, he thinks of a limb that has fallen asleep or when one goes to the dentist and gets a numbing shot to the mouth. One might also think of being freezing cold and losing some sensation in one's fingers and toes.

These are very similar to what I feel, but MS numbness also comes with pain. Let's take it a step further. Have you ever sat on the toilet so long that your legs and feet go numb and when you stand, you have weakness in your legs and movement is painful? You may stumble out of the restroom and have to be still or sit down until you get the feeling back.

This is very similar to MS numbness, but the good thing for you is that it goes away quickly. For an MS patient, this feeling may stay for days, weeks, months, even years. Like I said before, MS is very unpredictable…very!

Let me explain another example of what I have gone through.

On August 16, 2004, I played golf with my dad and his friends. Of course, I beat them. But this time, I beat them bad! This was the best round I have ever shot to this very day. I think I shot a 78. To say the least, I was excited and was on a high. It was the dead of summer and hot but not too bad.

MS Tip: most MS patients are severely affected by high temperatures. At this point in my dis-ease, I was not aware of this. That changed that day.

At that time of my life, I played a lot of golf. That particular day, we were playing on the north side of Houston, the same side of the city where my parents lived and where I grew up.

By this time, I had moved to the south side of Houston. After that awesome round of golf and since I was out that way, I visited my mother. As I drove to their home, I had a funny feeling on my right side. I was 26 and not really in-tune with my body, so I really did not know what was going on.

When I arrived at my parents' home, I got out of the car, but I felt slow and weak – a very different feeling to how I felt on the golf course. I knew something was not right. I greeted my mother; she was preparing a meal and I just so happened to get there at the right time. I love it when that happens! I shifted my thoughts from how I was feeling to the meal. I ate and ate well.

After the meal, as I was relaxing, I noticed that my right hand had become numb. I went into the kitchen and asked my mother to shake my hand.

We shook hands, and she asked me why was I shaking her hand with a dishrag? Ha! That is a southern phrase to describe someone with a weak grip.

I said, "Ok, how about this?" and we shook again.

She said it was the same. Then she asked what was I trying to do. I told her was trying to squeeze her hand as hard as I could, but my hand wasn't working. She was taken aback and told me to sit down and rest. After about an hour or so, I started feeling a tingling in my arm.

As that tingle moved up my arm, it left my hand totally paralyzed. My mother told me to stay there overnight. I really just wanted to go home and be in my own bed, but I stayed because I didn't know what was going to happen next.

MY NEAR FUTURE WAS UNKNOWN

I waited and worried about what to expect. I thought that I might get to the point of complete paralysis. Time would tell and by the end of the night, there was complete paralysis on the right side of my body. From my face down to my foot, there was no sensation or control. It was almost like I had a stroke, but on the right side.

This was new and I had to try to deal with the unknown as well as learn how to do things differently. This episode of paralysis lasted an entire month. Let me tell you what that month included: I stayed at my parents' home for the entire time and I had to file for short term disability from work. What's even more terrifying was, I was dealing with something for the first time on that level and when there is uncertainty, it wears on you.

In time, I could move around. I still had a lame arm and a lame leg. I tried to hop around and play it cool. I put my arm in a sling like I had an injury or surgery. I was eventually able to go home and get some supplies. It was strange seeing neighbors and waving with the opposite hand while walking with a limp.

I saw the bewildered and concerned look on their faces. They did not know that I had MS. Those who knew me a little asked what happened, and, of course, I told them. The others who did not ask treated me like I'd had a motorcycle wreck. They probably thought I was pulling an insurance scam. But still, I was just happy I could visit my home.

After the trip home, I returned to my parents' house for another two weeks. Another reason for the long stay was that I had not been cleared to drive. All of the paralysis happened on my right side — the driving side. As time passed, I regained the function of my foot, legs and arms. I was able to drive myself (against my mother's will) to the doctor and get officially cleared for driving.

Boy, can I tell you I have never felt that free in my life! I was able to drive home and wait in my house by myself. The truer freedom was getting better and not worrying if anything else was going to happen to me that week. I was getting back to normal, but I wasn't all the way normal yet. Being paralyzed on one side with parts that did not function properly, the left side of my body compensated for the lameness on the right side. This meant my gait was off.

Once I fully regained motion in my leg and feet, I had to re-learn how to walk. A normal person walks heel to toe and properly flexes their foot. However, after not using all the small muscles in my foot for so long, it was a foreign action.

For two months, I had to go to physical therapy to learn how to properly walk again. It was truly a struggle to just get back the Mike

Love walk. Needless to say, I made it through and the Mike Love walk is just as goofy as ever.

One of my motivations to get back to normal was getting a chance to play golf one more time. I was blessed to recover from that exacerbation fully and I still play golf – not as well as that day, but I still I play nonetheless. All that matters is that I can. When I think about one of my most life-impacting relapses, I think of this next one. It was the most painful and most revealing to me.

On July 10th, 2009, I proposed to my beautiful wife and all was peaceful and blissful. It was epic and if you see me one day just ask about that story. I pulled off a great proposal, I must say so myself. About a month later, we were now talking about our future and wedding plans, all that fun stuff. It was a Friday night and I was at her house. It was a low-key night — we were just hanging out and before you knew it we'd fallen asleep.

Around 11 pm, I woke up with a stomach that was tossing and turning, enough for me not to contain my dinner. As that happened, a severe dizzy spell came over me and I couldn't really walk. The room was spinning and I was trying to explain to the future Mrs. Love what and how I was feeling.

The feeling was so bad, I told her to take me to the hospital. All the while, I was still dizzy and throwing up. I got my senses back a little, but then it hit me. The most massive headache ever in the history of headaches. It was behind my left ear. There was a severe ringing in my ear and the room was spinning fast. I had no idea what was going on. Of course, my lady was scared and confused because she had no idea what was going on. I'm sure she grew more scared when I told her call an ambulance.

After another minute or two, I passed out on the floor. When I woke up, the headache was still there, so I just started crawling towards the front door in a small effort to get closer to the hospital. For one, I knew she could not carry me and if I was going to die, I didn't want to die in her lovely home. Considerate, right? I passed out again while crawling.

All of a sudden, I woke up and saw an angel and heard her calling my name, "Mike! Mike...."

I said, "Hey beautiful, don't I know you?"

She was so beautiful and I had to tell her right then and there.

My fiancé looked like an angel, but I was quickly brought back to reality when she told me, "Thank you, but this isn't the time for flirting."

Soon after that, the paramedics were at the door to pick me up off of the floor.

Off to the hospital I went.

We got to the hospital with all the bright lights and fuss that usually accompany an emergency. Questions were coming left and right and I could only halfway hear; I couldn't really see. But I did feel better knowing that I made it to the hospital.

They started an IV and I was getting stable. I told the night doctor that I had MS. Apparently, they didn't believe me because they wanted to do another spinal tap to make sure that this was an MS episode.

From the last chapter, we all know that I wasn't down for that again if I had a choice, especially to prove something I already knew. Thinking back on this now, I never knew you could be sick, in pain, feeling like you are about to die AND have anger run through your body. You may ask why I was angry. It was because they didn't believe me when I told them what was going on with this dis-ease.

Since I didn't let the random ER intern poke a hole in my spine, they gave me some morphine and sent my butt home.

Side note: one reason I wrote Micah's Story was to bring awareness to everyone, even **EMERGENCY ROOM CLINICIANS**! I'm not angry anymore. I can laugh at it now, but I wasn't doing a spinal tap again! No sir!

As I was being released from the hospital, my Mrs. Love was there. What was funny to me was that she'd called my parents that night and told them that I was being rushed to the hospital. I knew they were almost of the mind that 'He is your problem now!' but they did come and see me. I guess they knew more than we did. When I went home, I slept for at least ten hours. My body needed to recover from the trauma.

When I woke up, my girl was right there by my side. A few moments later, I had her sit on the side of the bed and told her that I wanted to talk to her. I told her that I loved her and that I was not sure how far this episode would go or how it would end. If she no longer wanted to get married, I would totally understand and didn't blame her if she had to rethink this whole for better or for worse thing. She took a second and had a slight angry look on her face. She took her pointer finger on her right hand and pointed it at me and said, "Don't ever tell me that again. I am here for you through it all."

Have you ever felt happy, relieved and even nervous all at the same time? The reason I was nervous was because I didn't know what she was going to do to me. I mean I couldn't defend myself at that time. I replayed the movie, *Misery* in my mind. The relieved part was that was the defining moment and I knew that I found my wife in Candice S. Coleman.

But as much as some things change, some things stay the same: I was back to boarding with my parents again. My mother was able to stay home and provide 'round the clock care. To this day, I still thank them every time I go to their home.

The next three to four weeks, Candice would come to my parents' house to see me every day after work. In Houston, that trip from the north side to the south is extreme; it's a haul. But she came every day; just to visit and take me for a ride in the car so I could get out of the house. That was a solid demonstration of 'for better or for worse'.

During this worse time, I began healing and getting back to normal. In the recovery phase, the nerves in my face went through a reconnection process and that was unreal. For a few weeks, my face around my eye and mouth drew up real tight. I was kind of like 'Two-Face' on Batman. One side was normal and the left side was smiling and winking. It looked very odd.

There was also a lot of twitching in some areas.It was all expected though; the amazing body was just in the healing process. Well, almost. Remember, sometimes with MS episodes, you may lose a function. As a result of that episode, I can't feel my left cheek to this day.

I also developed kidney stones. For anyone who has had kidney stones, you know exactly what I was going through. But I did not know what was going on. The pain just kept getting more and more severe in my side. I went back to the emergency room. Here we go again. This time it was a different pain and they kind of got it right. I got my meds and was sent home.

One of my medical angels is my primary care doctor, Dr. Angel Perez. He is the best, plus he is a great friend. I went into his office to follow-up on the kidney stones. All checked out and I went home, but later that afternoon, I called him because I hadn't gone to the restroom all day…and I mean all day! He told me to immediately go to the ER.

Here we go again. I was getting tired of this.

There was one ER nurse who was very active and on top of her game. She asked me when was the last time I went to the restroom. I told her it was the night before.

She said, "Ok, put this hospital robe on, I will be right back."

I followed her instructions and put on the hospital robe and lay on the bed.

At the time, my dad, who had driven me to the hospital, was standing next the bed on the left side. The nurse came back and told me to slide my feet up.

"Slide my feet up?" I asked.

"Yes, bend your knees," she responded.

I wasn't sure where this was going, but I did it. The hospital gown did what those always do…I was covered where I could see, but I felt a breeze and I knew that I was showing all of my 'yes ma'ams'!

I looked at my dad and he had the ' Oh shit' look on his face. I was about to ask him what was going on and then it happened. The nurse put a catheter in. I was lying there with the biggest what-the-hell and shocked look on my face. My dad had the 'I'm sorry' look on his face and the nurse was just smiling like she had just saved my life.

I asked her, "Lady, umm, what was that?" She told me I would be fine in a few seconds. I told her no I won't because she just took my manhood!

As she watched the urine bag fill, she seemed relieved. After I finished, she informed me that if I had produced another half an ounce of urine, my bladder would have erupted. I guess the smile on her face was true because she did save my life.

In this case, how do I spell relief? C-A-T-H-E-T-E-R! I left the hospital with a nice parting gift, a urine bag I had to wear for two weeks. Apparently, my prostate had become swollen from the kidney stones, which blocked my ability to urinate. But wait, that wasn't it! Just kidding, that was more than enough.

Now the road to recovery started again. The pee-bag was a little cool to me, believe it or not. It made going to the restroom very easy: just go in, dump, wash hands and roll out. I had to wear shorts all the time though. It's funny now as I think about it. But hey, I'm not complaining about that at all. I was able to get back to 98% normal (2% is my cheek and my taste buds on the left side of my tongue). So let's keep it moving!

I've always heard that if the dis-ease doesn't kill you, the treatment may. MS is a similarly compounding situation. After a subsequent episode of numbness from the waist down to my feet, I was prescribed was another round of high dose steroids. Over time I got better and life was again returning to normal. I was taking care of myself; doing what needs to be done. Even the simple stuff like hygiene, things that are so routine, were victories for me. However, little did I know that there would be another side illness from MS and the recovery steroid medication.

About a month after this last episode, I went to the dentist for pain in my lower left jaw. I thought it was a toothache/cavity, but it was more than that. It was an abscessed tooth. I know you are thinking like me, not now, not this, I have been through enough. "But, umm, yeah that's going to have to be pulled out Mr. Love," was all I heard.

Well, I'm not a baby so I was ready to get it done. They pulled the tooth and I was on my way, but for some strange reason, it was taking a long time for my gums to heal. Like more than a month!

I went back to the dentist because I was still in pain and the dentist was shocked it hadn't healed. He was aware of me having

MS and asked me what medication was I on at the time. There was a short list, but on the list, were the high dose steroids. He took an X-ray and immediately came back to me and said he was sending me to get a 3D X-ray, because it may be more severe than he'd originally thought. He also took a swab of the affected area. Then I was let go with orders to come back the next day after the X-ray.

When I returned the next day he confirmed what he was thinking. He told me that I have osteomyelitis in my jaw. I was like, "What's that?"

That's when he told me it was a bone-eating bacteria! I was informed that if I didn't get it taken care of soon, I may lose my entire jaw. WHAT?!?!

By then, Candice and I were married, so of course, she was the first person I called. I told her what was going on and she was floored. I was thinking the same thing. As you may know, I'm the 'find out a problem, then ok, how do we fix it' person. She asked how I got it.

Here is the strange part that you never see coming.

After the tooth was pulled and while I was on the high dose steroids from the previous MS exacerbation, I continued to brush my teeth as normal person. Twice a day, up, down, round and round, perfect angle, all of that.

Well, little did I know that the act of brushing your teeth can introduce bacteria into your mouth. While this is not normally a problem for a healthy person, I was on the high dose steroids which stripped my white blood cells' ability to fight the bacteria. Even brushing my teeth was a problem! Yeah, I know, it's a super roundabout way of almost losing your jaw, but this is what I was dealing with.

I saw another specialist and surgery was in order. They had to remove another tooth and bone in my jaw to make sure that all of the bacteria was gone. They also had to do a bone graft to restore the structure in my jaw. Major, major surgery.

I was in the hospital for four days, in a semi-sterile environment to prevent the reintroduction of more bacteria. When it was all said and done, I ended up with two dental implants. From the start of this process until the end, it took a full three years to properly heal and enjoy chewing a steak again. If anyone offers me a steak dinner or even a stick of gum, I'm game. Don't be mad if I take two!

CHAPTER FOUR

I Need Help, But Not Really

The week after I was diagnosed with MS, the doctor wanted me to come in for a follow-up. We were going to check on things like my mental state, what might happen in the future, how to take or, rather, give myself the medications every day.

It was the official 'here you go… go live your life with this and call me if you need me… maybe?' Little did I know that this visit was going to be the turning point in the way I viewed my life with this illness and the beginning of my vow to defeat it.

I was at the door. I took a deep breath and I walked into the doctor's office. There was one row of about eight chairs in the middle of the room. There were people in the room but, strangely, no one was sitting in the chairs. On one end to the left was a woman in a wheelchair. She was a pretty lady. She had a smart look with small frame glasses. She looked athletic and had an encouraging, inviting smile – the kind of smile that could get you to give her more than you wanted to.

On the other end of the eight chairs was a man in a wheelchair. He had on nice cowboy boots, jeans and a pearl snap shirt. His short haircut was reminiscent of a military cut. His face seemed to be focused and determined, with eyes that were a little squinty and showed tan marks from where he wore his sunglasses. He looked like a working man. Then again, he was in a wheelchair.

As I took a seat in one of the middle chairs, I heard the man and woman conversing about their similar experiences. Since there was just three of us, they included me in the conversation. We did the regular 'Hi, how are you doing?' stuff but then they were very forward with me.

The first question the lady asked me was, "Are you here because you have MS?"

I said, "Yes ma'am, I sure am."

The man asked me how long I'd had it. I told him I was diagnosed a week ago, but I guess I'd had it longer than that. Both responded with somber, sorry looks on their faces. I could tell they felt sorry for me.

Then there was a strange, almost deafening silence in the waiting room. I felt like I needed to ask questions, so I asked, "Before you both were diagnosed, what did you do, career-wise? What was your daily routine or activity?"

The man said he worked for South Western Bell and climbed telephone poles to fix lines. He was active before his diagnosis the year before. Once he found out he had MS, he'd gone into a depression, became still and just let the dis-ease do what it was going to do. He pointed to the wheelchair and told me that that is what MS had done. I turned the compassion they showed me back to him.

I then turned to the lady and asked her the same questions. She said she was an aerobics instructor and experienced a similar thing when she was diagnosed: she went into a depression and took a break from instructing aerobics.

"And this is where I am now," she said pointing down to her wheelchair. She asked me how old I was and I told her I was twenty.

They both shook their heads and said, "So young."

I was like, "Wait a minute! Am I about to die?"

They both said no but indicated that they knew how I would eventually end up. I asked her if they were psychic?

"Of course not," the lady said, "but we were two active people and look how MS has ruined our lives."

I slumped back into my seat into another deafening silence. This time, it was because I was thinking.

The nurse broke the silence and said, "Micah, you can come in now." When I stood up, I told the lady and the man thank you. They both had bewildered looks on their faces as I walked to the office. Like them, I'm sure you're wondering why I said thank you. I can distinctively remember this as a defining moment for me as an MS patient.

It was my ah-ha moment! Out of that short conversation, I was able to get a few points on what not to do.

The first was not to get depressed because I was chosen to have MS. Somehow, I would make this a blessing to others.

The second thing was not to give up on myself. I would continue to live my life. Fully. Those two people were over-active before they were diagnosed, but then they gave up and let MS take them where it wanted to take them.

I have always believed that if you control your mind and serve the Almighty God, **ANYTHING IS POSSIBLE!**

Let me be clear, I don't want to take anything away from my fellow brothers and sisters in this MS fight. For many, it is more than mind over matter and being limited to a wheelchair is not a choice. There are four different severities of MS:

- **Relapsing-Remitting:** relapses occur for limited periods and new and varied symptoms may occur with each relapse. This is also the most common type of MS

- **Secondary Progressive:** relapses or remissions may occur along with symptoms that progressively worsen over time

- **Primary Progressive:** no relapses or remissions occur but symptoms progressively worsen over time. This occurs in about 10% of MS patients

- **Progressive Relapsing:** affecting about 5% of MS patients, this type sees the condition of the patient steadily worsen. Relapses with no remissions occur

Of the four types, I suffer from the least severe, Relapsing-Remitting. Knowing this made me hopeful about my ability to maintain my quality of life. For those suffering from the other types, they are and will always be the superheroes of MS warriors.

As I noted before, the main thing I got from talking with those two, was to never give up on myself, and take the chance to be great. Life will always have its swings and changes; we just have to be flexible and change and redirect along with it. We have to be fluid like water and fill the spaces in our lives with love. Fill it like water in a dry parking lot. Gather where the low spots are and fill the holes with more love! Ok, sorry about that rant.

Back to those two people: they allowed me to see the fork in my road. I could have been idle and who knows where this MS thing could have and would have gone? From that day on, I took the small steps that I do every day to take control of my life. Many days I am feeling the best, and sometimes it makes me wonder if this is the start to an end. So, I pray for those two and thank God for allowing them to cross my path and give me that experience to learn from. They didn't know they started something in me. They started a fire that could never be put out.

I've also had to work through negative 'advice', sometimes from those closest to me. These are the people who you think would give the most support when you are trying to do anything positive for yourself. Of course, the bad advice or lack of support was all because they loved me. All they wanted to do was just protect me. Maybe they thought that because I was in a fragile body that I'd have to 'take it easy'. That I shouldn't do too much. That I should avoid overextending myself. I totally understand that mindset, but if I chose to listen to that all the time, I would just sit and watch life go by.

Then, my life would go and my spirit would go bye-bye with it. This is a belief I had to stand on while I bucked the system. I wanted to change my disaster into a delight and all I need most days are for people to give me a little support or just a nod to say they are behind me. I love having a small cheering crowd to push me.

This brings me back to when I decided to face the challenge of the BP MS 150. Most so-called healthy people would think it's crazy to ride a bike for 150 miles over two days. Given that I have MS, they would think I'm double-crazy. But not me. I figured, hey, why not do it when I can help others and myself in the process. It was a cause that was close to my heart.

You know how, in your circle, you have those who support you no matter what and those who aren't quite sure? Those who say 'Hey, I'm not sure that's a good idea'? There are several reasons the naysayers behave that way, I think.

For one, they may feel that they could never pull off what I want to accomplish. They may not be motivated to do anything bold in life and are rather happy (or complacent) with the 'norm'. But I still ask myself, "Why not and why not me?" For that reason, in my quest to be extraordinary (or at the very least, 'normal'), I have to pick and choose who I share my adventures with. What category are you in? Are you willing to come with me?

CHAPTER FIVE

God's Plan

"Your eyes saw my unformed body; all the days ordained for me were written in your book before one of them came to be."

— Psalm 139:16

All my days were written in my book of life before even one of them was fulfilled! This verse has allowed me to be where I am physically and mentally with MS.

Many times I am asked how I keep going, how I look so well with MS, what's my secret. I really have no secret; but I have the truth. The first part of the truth is I have no control over MS and MS has no control over me. The second part of the truth is, I know who is in control of me and MS. This Bible verse suggests that all of this — my life, the direction I go, you reading this book — has already been planned by the Creator. In me accepting that I am not the captain of my ship, life seems a little less stressful.

Over time, I discovered that the main triggers for relapses were extreme temperatures, diet and stress. Stress was number one. When I turned the corner and took control of my MS in 2005, I was single and had just purchased a home in a rapidly growing area in South Houston called Pearland. It was a great area for a middle class, young professional. That time of my life was a lot of fun but it also had its own levels of stress. I'd moved straight out of my parents' home into a three-bedroom, two-bathroom home. It was a big jump for a 25-year-old.

I remember one random week when life as a person with MS hit me and I was having a flare-up. I was not really feeling well, but I was still moving around, going to work, working out and doing the 25-year old thing. By that Thursday, I was still not feeling 100% but I told myself, "Self, let's go out!"

At that time in my life, I knew where all the spots were in Houston. I mean, aaaalllll the spots! On Thursdays, there was a spot called the M Bar that hosted a party called Milkshake. Milkshake was the hottest party in Houston and even though I knew I wasn't feeling that well, I had to get out of the walls of my new house. I knew I needed someone to roll with me, so I called the person I trusted the most, my boy Ian! I had a short conversation with him about what was going on. Ian likes to party too, so I knew we were going to have a great time.

I took a nap, got up, got dressed and it was on! I picked up Ian at his house. He and his wife, Frene', lived in the same neighborhood. We talked on our way to the party, keeping it light and fun as usual. We arrived, and I ran into my other buddy, Brandon, also known as B. Nawf! It was a great combination of party people and as I walked into the spot, I forgot all about my MS flare-up.

All of the pain, numbness and tingling was left in the car. I had a great time. There were libations, conversation, music and pretty women — how could any 25-year old single guy think of MS and its effects when all of that was going on?

It was great; just what the doctor ordered. Well, not exactly what he ordered, but it worked nonetheless. We stayed out late and went to eat afterwards before heading back home. As I drifted off to sleep that night, I realized I was feeling just fine. No numbness...nothing!

It was almost like another ah-ha moment. If I were to focus on what was wrong, then I would never get right. I'd probably get worse.

From that point on, I was able to find all the basic stresses in my life. Most of them I realized I was causing myself. The new home was one of them. Being on an overly strict health regimen was another. You know when you get orders from a doctor to follow this and follow that without deviation or you will suffer bad consequences? That in itself causes stress!

It's great having people in your life who care for you, but when they tell you that you should not do something or to get rest even though you are not tired and to just change who you are, that causes stress! I had to get those small triggers under control. I eventually found out what worked for me. I would take my medicine but, other than that, I would just live my life and have fun. That was a game changer for me.

Let's get back to Psalm 139:16. We can only control so much in life. If we leave it all in the hands of God, the Creator, all will be handled properly.

As the verse says, the book of your life has been written already. So staying home and being extra cautious about something you can't control is kind of dumb, right? If you trust God, focus and seek ye first His kingdom, all things will be added unto you. What things, you ask? All the things you want, including good health. I stand on that. He hasn't failed me and I predict that He never will.

This thinking has allowed me to do extraordinary things in my life over the past fifteen years. This includes being married and having children. It seems that loving your life should be an easy, automatic thing, but it was a real consideration I had to examine before I went on my pursuit of happiness.

When I was diagnosed, I had serious doubts about having children. Here is the reason: I believe that the MS condition is passed through the genes. Medical professionals do not agree on this point, and while it is true that not all children inherit the defect, I have several cousins on the same side of my family who have MS (shout out to my kinfolks!). That tells me that there is some genetic component to this.

So how do you stop the gene from spreading? Well, just stop spreading the gene. Do not reproduce, right? Simple. There it is, there is the plan. No problem. Well, there is a problem. Doing that goes against the mindset of being fluid with your universe and moving around obstacles and continuing on.

I remember being with my best friend, his wife and my future wife at the time. Ian and Frene had a three-year-old and an almost one-year-old. I watched and observed the happiness they had together. They functioned as a family. We were in the park and it was flat-out fun. Not a kicking-it type of fun, but a fun you can't pay for.

The three-year-old was running around just being in the now, and the almost one-year old was looking around trying to figure out where she was. Where is this place? What was this green stuff on the ground? Grass! Just simply grass. We were joined by another great friend of mine who had a five-year-old and three-year-old. They were at a different stage in the family cycle, but it was still fun.

As I sat back and watched these two families enjoy the simple things, I realized that I wanted the same. This happiness was not bought, they were blessed with it. I still had in the back of my mind the harm I could cause by passing on my MS gene. As I talked to one of the mothers, I mentioned how expensive I thought kids could be. She agreed, but she looked me straight in the eye and told me that the joy they brought on a daily basis was worth it. That was the part that got me.

She settled into her thoughts and said, "But Micah, you know what? God has provided all that we need and has never come up short. He gave us the blessing and responsibility to raise these children. He knows what is good and what we can handle. He gifted us these children to go forward to expand His kingdom through this family. So, money is not an issue God can't handle."

I understood in my heart every word she said. What she said sunk in and it really helped me move past the small thinking I was having about not having children. I know the real reason for me saying that was not about the money. Money is a temporary issue that may be in front of me or anyone.

The real issue was me not trusting that God can handle any situation, including MS. I really didn't want to pass on something that I knew in my heart was uncomfortable or that could cause severe or debilitating pain. This was something that bothered me for years. However, after that conversation, I renewed my mind and came to grips with it. I realized that I had to trust in God to handle all my uncertainties.

Another major concern was if I'd be healthy enough to raise a child. For many years, I reflected on that conversation and was able to come to the conclusion that I was tripping. I was doubting that the ALMIGHTY God, the creator of the universe was not able to handle my itty bitty MS problem.

Once I stopped trying to rewrite my book of life, it freed me up to enjoy the best things in life. Now I have two wonderful sons and I look forward to their future. I am very optimistic on how bright their futures will be. As of this writing, they are four-years old and eight-months old. They are the delight of my life. I can just imagine what I would have missed if I had stayed blind and dumb and did not trust God to handle everything, including this very impactful and important thing. It all started with the renewing of my mind and knowing who I belong to and who is in control, the almighty God.

By me establishing a renewed trust in God, it opened doors that I never imagined. I yearn to learn more about Jesus Christ, which allows me to get closer to God and see even more things from His great plan for me.

I have to be honest, I have quite often asked God to take this from me. But as I read the Word, I am directed and motivated by it and I trust God to do with me as He may.

CHAPTER SIX

God's Plan II, Hindsight

As you get older, you may hear the phrase, "If I knew then what I know now...." Of course, we would all be rich or a so-called better person. If you are a Bible reader, you may have heard Romans 8:28 which reads, *"And we know that in all things God works for the good of those who love him, who have been called according to his purpose."*

In reality, when we are in the middle of going through something, it's hard to process why something has happened. We think it's not fair. We wonder what happened and what could we have done differently to have a different outcome. At the same time, we try to figure how to make the situation better. We may also have to face that there is nothing we can do about it. It is done, it's a wrap! This often happens with life-changing situations like when someone dies unexpectedly or you lose a great job or someone leaves your life or you're diagnosed with some strange dis-ease.

In my case, it was this dis-ease. Now, I don't want to take away from someone who has been diagnosed with a life-ending dis-ease. Pause. On many occasions, I have seen people beat the so-called end date set for them by doctors. So please, don't give up! Put your faith in the one and only Lord and Savior Jesus Christ. Read my favorite life verse in the Bible, Ephesians 3:20, *"Now to him who is able to do immeasurably more than all we ask for or imagine, according to his power that is a work within us."* This is the miracle you have to believe in.

Ok, back to your regular scheduled program. Where was I? Oh yeah... when I was diagnosed in 1999, I first had to figure out what the hell MS was. Being the person I am, if there is a problem, I'm all about finding a solution and going with it. It was not that simple in this situation.

With MS, there is a huge medical component, but, as I've shown, there are also mental and spiritual components. To be honest, I grasped these very slowly. Maybe slower than others and I'm still a work in progress. Remember, I was around twenty years old when I was diagnosed. I will be forty by the time you read this. So be patient, to say the least. Outside all of that, I still have to survive.

At times I had to forget what I was going through; other times I had to focus on not giving in to the suffering. The forgetting part was hard to do at times. A numb arm, leg, and face can be hard to ignore, but the sooner I was able to free my mind, the sooner I was able to overcome. While going through that process, many things happened, but over time, I was in the position to appreciate hindsight.

I was able to learn and better equip myself for the next challenge.

When I was diagnosed in 1999, I was well on my way to graduating and going to the Air Force Academy and the eventually on to being a commercial airline pilot. I was scheduled to graduate in the spring of 2000, but I faced a few speed bumps which pushed my graduation date to 2001. Who knows what my life would have been if I'd graduated on time and the plan went as I'd envisioned.

Fast forward to fall 2001 on September 11th. I would have been a year and a half in the armed forces. I would likely have been pushed into the middle of a war. Did MS actually save my life? Was hindsight actually showing me a gift of fate? Maybe, maybe not.

There is also the question of who I married. Before I was married I was dating of course, and not really sure about with who or when I would settle down. I was interested in someone I could have married, someone who I thought could be perfect. I tried to make her perfect for me. She was fully aware of me having MS and what could possibly happen at any given moment. As time went on, I eventually had an MS relapse. It was one of the debilitating ones. I was out for about a month. Paralysis happened and I was not sure how far it was going to go or how long it was going to last.

The very weekend it happened, I was scheduled to hang with the fellas in Austin, Texas. I couldn't go. All of the crew I was rolling with said that if I couldn't go, they wouldn't either. I thought that was an honorable thing for them to do. Yes, I have great friends. However, this lady I was 'seriously' dating got a call from her friends to go to the same event. She decided to go. I didn't try to stop her; I actually encouraged her to go.

We were not married and I accepted that I was not her number one priority. To be fair, she may have needed to get away. As I sat home, I was going through the mental anguish of how much, how long and how far this episode would go. I'm sure she thought of that too. That's probably why she went to the party — to get away from the madness. It wasn't her duty to nurse me back to health, but after she returned, things were just not the same. I'm sure she did not want a part of that life.

That is totally understandable, and I've never held that against her. But I had to look at that as a save from getting married to someone who could not handle me and my dis-ease. It also freed me up to meet and get to know the woman I have now. And she's the truth.

There are also the unexpected 'benefits' of having this dis-ease. Many situations happen to me now because of MS, including having the opportunity to meet the MOST awesome staff at the National

MS Society in Houston. I'm not sure if this is the same of all the societies, but if you ever have the chance to visit a location, this is the one to visit. I often stop there to get a pick me up. The opportunity to be around just good, positive and authentic people. They don't know it, but that is my MS safe-haven. They allow me to be me and tell my story.

They have heard Micah's Story many times and it seems like they enjoy it every time. I have to give them a huge shout out and special thank you.

CHAPTER 7

Ridin' Dirty for Life

It was 4:00 am and I was up eating a cinnamon raisin bagel with peanut butter on it. I was getting enough protein and carbs to last me awhile. But again…why was I doing this?

Let's go back a few months. While driving down I10, headed west from Beaumont Texas, with a brand-new road bike in the back seat listening to UGK, I made one phone call.

I called Calvin Taylor. He usually cracks a joke first. After he did, I broke the news to him that I'd just bought a road bike. The conversation stopped. I was on the phone but thought I lost him because he was so quiet. He was quiet because I told him to give me a heads-up when he was going to start training for the BP MS 150.

At some point he told me, "You can tell who is serious about riding when they buy a bike!"

So I was serious. And excited.

Calvin told me that if I rode, he would ride again. Being the man of his word, he had to get his mind right to ride in it another year, which is not an easy task.

I got the bike home, still excited. My wife was excited too. She said that she was happy that I was officially doing something about something that affected me in such a major way. To this day, she has supported me to the max. Now, who remembers the days when you rode a bike as a child? You just hop on and roll? What's that old saying 'It's like riding a bike', right? Well, yes and no. This was not prepping for a Sunday ride in the park. There was some significant training in my future.

I proceeded to recruit some of my best friends for the journey. At midday on a Tuesday, I called my best buddy, Ian.

This is how the conversation went:

"This is Ian."

This was the usual, professional way he answers the phone. To this day, I don't know how to feel about this. He should have my number saved in his phone by now, right? He should know it's me, right? The professionalism should be out the door, right? Well, that's Ian.

Anyway, I said, "Hey homeboy!"

"Mister man, mister man, what's up!?"

"Hey, Ian, I need a big favor."

"Sure anything. Whatcha need?"

Then I hung up the phone! That is how you get friends to join you in an awesome, but seemingly impossible task. When I eventually told him the details, he jumped right in.

On the Friday evening before the first training ride, we were comparing notes and getting ready. We thought it was a good idea to have a bunch of supplies and gear. After all, I am an Eagle Scout. Be prepared! Well, yes, but you still had to prepare the right way and we didn't quite get it right.

We had so much stuff: a Camelback, extra snacks, long sleeve workout gear (I was a little chilly) and shorts to wear on top of spandex. The normal bike riding outfit is all spandex, top and bottom, but being the manly guys that we are, we felt it was a little, ummm say, revealing, to wear all spandex.

On that Saturday morning, we joined up with Calvin and a guy who rides bikes in triathlons and competitions. That day rain was in our forecast. Being the newbies that we were, we thought we were not going to ride. That was not the case. Calvin told us that if it was raining on the day of the MS 150, chances are we would still have to ride, so we might as well get used to it.

We started the ride with our extra shorts, long sleeve workout gear and Camelback. Before we started, Calvin suggested that we leave the Camelbacks and take off the long sleeves and the shorts. We would eventually appreciate the life lesson of listening to someone who's done it before. Anyway, we kept all the stuff as we begun the 60-mile ride.

We started out enjoying the training. The route took us through the west side of Houston, which has a few rolling hills and great scenery of cows in the countryside. Before long, however, the clouds turned gray and rain started to fall. This was around mile twenty-five. We had almost forty more miles to go with all of our wet stuff on: the Camelbacks, the long sleeve workout gear and the shorts. Oh, and did I mention the snacks we were carrying? All of that probably added eight pounds on our backs, which was a different training within itself.

As we were riding, it got to the point of being miserable. We were tired and hurting. If you haven't ridden a bike in a long time and then, suddenly, you ride long distance, you will have problems with your hind side. I wouldn't say problems, but you will have soreness. It's the type of soreness you've never had before. Even now, after riding for many years, I know I must put in enough time in the seat for me not to be uncomfortable. I also know that an experienced rider builds up a tolerance because my butt does not get as sore as it did when I first started. It's the way I know if I'm ready to ride or not – can I still feel my butt?

The lessons Calvin taught us that weekend were:

1. Wear the least amount of gear.

2. Put no extra weight on your back.

Nowadays, me and Ian are very comfortable in our manhood and we go all spandex! We understand the payoff in the end.

This first bike ride was more than we imagined, but it was a good baptism into the bike world. One thing about the MS 150 is you also have to train a lot on your own. One weekend, I decided to go on a ride by myself. My goal was to go for at least twenty miles. Before doing so, I realized few things: I needed to learn all safety protocol, how to change a flat tire, the correct balance of nutrition and discover a pace that was right for me.

Once I completed all of that, I started out on my solo journey. My tires were aired up properly, I had on the correct clothes and I had all the snacks and water I needed. I also had music going to get me pumping. With the music blaring and my shades and helmet on, it was time to attack the road.

By the time I hit the main highway I was warmed up and tuned to the right music station. R&B is what gets me into a groove. People make fun of me and ask why I don't play faster, more upbeat songs. I'd long figured out that if I played faster songs, I would try to pedal to that beat for the whole ride. That would wear me out faster and I needed to preserve energy.

However, if I slowed it down a bit, I would be able to ride for the long haul. Anyway, I was out rolling to my R&B mix and life was great. I did body checks and all was well. I looked down and saw that I was rolling at a pace of 20 to 23 mph. Now, for an amateur, that is humping it! I calculated my ride time. At 20 mph I'd be done in an hour, +/- a few minutes. This was going to be a breeze. Remember the word 'breeze'.

There are few things you can't truly predict or calculate when starting out like the wind!

When I reached the halfway mark, I decided to take a water break and eat a light snack. It was time to head back. However far I'd ridden, I'd have to ride back. Since I was taking the same path back, I knew I would see the same scenery, but this time, something was very different.I quickly realized that I was rolling so fast earlier because I had a good tailwind! I knew this because I faced a severe headwind on the way back.

If I had to choose, I think I would choose the headwind first, then the tailwind. This was not a fight I was planning on that day, but I had to get home. I got tight on my bike and prepared to fight through it. In my head, a headwind is like when you're playing with a child who is trying to hit you, but you are holding him back by his head. He may continue to swing and fight, but he is getting nowhere. Nevertheless, he will keep trying and, like that kid, I had to knuckle up and keep trying. This made me really hate the wind.

As I rode, I checked how strong the wind was blowing and from which direction it was coming. During that ten-mile ride home, I didn't realize how happy I'd be to see a red light. To be honest, I didn't even remember the red lights during the front half of my ride. But coming back, I enjoyed each and every one of those mandatory breaks. I was trying to catch all the red lights! That wind was so real!

My fight with the wind happened often during our training rides, but it prepared me for what I had in store. Our team trained for about five months. Very few of us knew exactly to expect during the big ride so we took every opportunity to train.

As time passed, we became stronger and faster and team 'Ridin' Dirty truly started to come together. As I mentioned, the first to join was Ian. He was a physical thrill challenge junkie and loved this kind of stuff. Calvin, the one who introduced me to cycling, was next to jump in. He had been my first boss out of college and I credit him for ruining my work ethic. At the very least, he made me a very efficient worker. At work he would always ask, "Why are you doing all of that?" Translated, that meant 'why do it in eight hours, when you can do it in four and chill for the rest?'. The next to join was a friend of Calvin's, Antoinette, who we affectionately called 'AZ'. She was the team's only girl, the team's sweetheart. She gave our predominately male team a different perspective and she kept us laughing.

Over time, the training rides became more organized and purposeful. I never knew the bike world until I got involved with this. It is a whole different world. I tell people it is a world where all the hippies grew up, needed to make money to support their families, but still wanted to have fun and keep their lifestyle. So they figured, hey, let's ride bikes and sell bike stuff and from that all the bike shops grew. The next time you walk into your local bike shop, get to know the people and then tell me what you think.

The bike world is also a huge family. Everybody is willing to help and help you get better.It's a great atmosphere. Organized rides are often sponsored by bike shops and those who support and follow them. They call them supported rides. When you are part of a supported ride, you have police protection, established breakpoints and snacks! Our team signed up for a few of these supported rides.

Along with the camaraderie, these rides helped us get over any fears of riding with people or in a crowd. If you know me, you know that I enjoy this way more than riding alone but to some new riders, it could be intimidating. There's really nothing to be afraid of. People and bikes are not stacked on top of each other like what you see on TV during the Tour De France.

There is plenty of room and just like when you're in a car, you can either speed up or slow down to get more room. During the training season, Ridin' Dirty completed around seven of these supported rides. After training for months, I'd become stronger, faster and I had gotten most of the kinks out of my bike. Before I knew it, it was late April and time to ride.

Back to 4:00 a.m. and me eating a cinnamon raisin bagel with peanut butter on it. I was getting enough protein and carbs to last me awhile. I was not sure when I would eat again, but I knew I needed the fuel. The night before, I'd prepared my Ridin' Dirty uniform, all the while being nervous like an athlete before a big race. I still had some of that nervous energy as I walked out the house to secure my bike to the back of my car. I was ready to hit the road.

As I drove west, it was still dark. The further I drove, the more I started seeing bikes strapped to the back or on top of vehicles. It was like we all were going to battle. Well, in my mind, the ride was a battle. I was getting excited — I was in a super zone. I had to watch myself because the more excited I got, the faster I started driving.

I got to the team's meeting spot and got out of the car feeling good, pumped and ready to ride. Everyone made last minute bike checks, filled up their water bottles, got their snacks together and took the supplements we needed. We circled up for a word of prayer and then got rolling. It was a great feeling when everyone was finally rolling, especially after all of those months of training. We were out for our great adventure and having this team by my side along with the extended behind-the-scenes members is what really made this first ride special for me.

Ridin' Dirty was on the move!

During the first five miles, you get the kinks out. Eventually, you get your music right, you crack jokes — well the jokes went on for the whole ride — and you also begin to experience the magic of interacting with other riders. There are constant transitions during the ride, so you may ride next a stranger for miles before finding yourself next to someone entirely new for the next few miles.

For most of the ride, teams cluster together. Our team had already agreed on how fast we would ride and which rest stops we would visit. However, once you get on the road, it's funny how plans change and it was not uncommon for us to separate for a few miles. We still coordinated on break points, stopping when we needed to or passing one if we felt good, but when we were riding, our team mixed with others.

That is when I had the most fun. The MS Society provides people who have MS with a special jersey. It has a distinctive design and printed on it are the words 'I Ride Because I Have MS.' I was proud to wear that jersey because it was my testimony and, I believe, a motivation to others.

I figured they'd see it and think, hey if he is riding and he has MS, why can't I suck it up and ride it out? It also allowed me to have conversations with tons of strangers. If you know me, I'm never lonely and I remember a few of those interactions very well. One in particular showed me how unpredictable life was.

I was riding next to a young lady that was just cruising along. She spoke and I spoke back. She had what I thought was an Australian accent and when I asked to confirm she happily said, "Yes, yes, I am from Australia." She had come over to ride in honor of her sister who was diagnosed about five years prior. I told her how special and amazing I thought it was that she had traveled that far for this ride. I thanked her.

As we continued to talk she mentioned that she had not been cycling long, but wanted to do something special for her sister. About a month before the ride, while training, she begun to not feel well and decided to see a doctor. She went through many tests, which all eventually indicated that she too had MS. Her diagnosis did not stop her training. Now she was riding for two people, her sister and herself.

That story motivated me to keep going during the ride; to keep pedaling and pushing – for me and for her. I realized something about myself: I get satisfaction when I am serving others. I was as motivated to serve her as I was to ride for myself. Christ's instruction to treat thy neighbor as you would treat yourself resounded in my head and this became my secret to having peace in my heart during that ride.

During that first day, we encountered a brutal headwind. By the end of our training rides, we were averaging 16-17 mph, which is pretty good. With that headwind, however, we were slowed to 8-10 mph. After about four and a half hours into the ride, Ian rolled up on my left side. He had that look on his face. It was a look that said 'man what did you get me into?'. He didn't even have to say a word before I responded, "Man, my bad. I'm sorry! I didn't know it was like this!" He busted out with the huge laugh and said, "Let's go homie. I got ya!" This was all I needed to push through that headwind.

That first day took us nine whole hours to make it to the halfway point at La Grange, TX. As we rolled into La Grange, there was a super warm welcome as we crossed the finish line. I was exhausted and elated to make it there but I soon felt that I was starting to have an MS relapse. I sat down at our RV campsite and could not move. I stayed in the same folding chair for three hours. The rest of the team showered and ate.

I could feel the numbness starting to take over my entire body. I may have pushed myself a little too much, but at least I made it. After resting some more, I soon began to recover. I got up and was able to function. I showered quickly (I'm sure everyone was happy I did) and ate a great meal. I went to sleep and was probably one level away from being in a coma. You know the kind of sleep when you wake up in the same position you fell asleep in? Yes, I was dead sleep! That was some of the best rest I'd had in a long time. I woke up the next morning ready to roll.

The next day, I wasn't looking forward to riding as much as I was the first day. The hardest part was getting back on the seat after nine hours of riding the first day. There was some soreness, but that wasn't the main issue. Remember my numbness from the night before? By the time I woke up, I really couldn't feel my legs. I quickly turned my minor relapse into a positive!

You see, I couldn't feel my legs, but I could still use them. In not having much feeling, I also couldn't feel the pain when tackling the hills into Austin. No one else knew why I wasn't struggling with discomfort the way they were. I was riding like a madman. I can remember going up one of the steepest, longest hills.

I was passing people and yelling, "People! Let's go!" I was the annoying, pumped guy with the 'I ride with MS' shirt on. I passed an older lady slowly working her way up the hill.

When I was passed her I said, "Ma'am this hill ain't shit!"

Shortly after, I heard some gears shift and she yelled back, "You are right, this hill isn't shit!"

Everybody around us laughed and we pushed on.

We got through the mind-boggling hills to be greeted by one of the strongest side winds we had to deal with. It was hard to keep the bike on the road. There were only fifteen or so miles to go and we were too close to stop now. We pushed on, encountering hill after hill after hill.

Break points had become lifesaving stops and my body was telling me it was time to get off the bike; my mind agreed. About four miles outside the last rest stop, the whole team was out of water. The sun was out now, the temperature has risen and water was scarce on the road. During less important rides, this may have been a legitimate reason to call it quits. But we were too close to stop now, right?

We spent the least amount of time at the last rest stop. We were in and out quickly. We all just wanted to make it to the finish line and get the hell off our bikes! When we hit the road again and got closer to city limits, the momentum began to build. Excitement and adrenaline were starting to kick in. As we approached downtown Austin, the highway turn into streets with stop lights, we were riding alongside traffic and the buildings got bigger. This got us super pumped because we knew the end was near.

We started to see lots of burnt orange as we rode by the University of Texas. The excitement kept building. I made a few more turns and saw that the streets were starting to fill with people. It was getting louder. We made the last left-hand turn on to a street lined with hundreds of people. There was music and an announcer encouraging us in on the loudspeaker. I looked up and saw a sign that read 'FINISH'.

At that moment, it seemed that we had only just passed the start sign. But, truthfully, there was so much that had happened since then. There were so many stories, so many jokes, so many... everything. We had embarked on the journey together. We'd held tight, helped each other and ended strong. It's amazing, how powerful a few positive words from your teammate can push you along; I truly valued having the right people to push me further and harder.

I realized that we had accomplished two things. One, we had met the challenge of riding from Houston to Austin on bicycles. Two, we had fully supported a great cause that represented myself and all of my fellow MS warriors all over the world. For most of my team, I was the only person who they personally knew with the dis-ease and yet, they had supported countless others.

As we approached the finish line, I could see and hear hundreds of people cheering us in. Since I was wearing the 'I Ride Because I Have MS' jersey, it seemed like the cheers went up an octave or two as I passed. We crossed the line giving each other high-fives and feeling super excited to be done.

As we rode past the finish line, I slowed down a little to allow the team go ahead of me. I was choked up and didn't want them to see that. I realized that these people loved me enough to go through hell and no water to support my effort to overcome MS. If you want to experience sacrifice, just jump on a bike and ride 150 miles.

I don't know how to repay these people.

All I can say is thank you over and over again. They are all examples of great friends.

We play together, we pray together, we ride together, and we will always be…..

Ridin' Dirty for life.

CONCLUSION

In my life, I have learned that you lose things. You lose hair, teeth, money, creature comforts and business. However, the most valuable things you could lose are unseen. They are things like love, time, trust, hope, friendship, motivation, drive, direction and health. The funny thing is, the most valuable things can't be bought. We scratch and claw our way through life trying to purchase tangible things that perish with their use. But if you think about it, we would not be able to fully enjoy those tangible things if those valuable, priceless and unseen things weren't in place.

As you've read in Micah's Story, I've lost, teeth, hair, some health, friends and the chance to pursue opportunities that could have changed my life. However, I have learned to live my life one day at a time. I don't fear the future because I have limited control over it and I am a child of God. He has mapped it out for me already so all I can do is live and trust. I also rarely have regrets. Yesterday is over and it's history. I try my best to live in the now and focus on the present. My truth is that I'm still here, so I can still do...do whatever.

Thank you for lending me your time and attention.
Let's continue in the fight to win.

1 love

This story will be continued....

Micah's Story

RIDIN' DIRTY ADVENTURES

Myself (Micah Love) & Stacie Kover-Kuskie

"EXPERIENCE THE FREEDOM!"

Ridin' Dirty riding with PURPOSE.

Ridin' Dirty's TREK FROM HOUSTON, TX to AUSTIN, TX!

Made in the USA
Columbia, SC
12 September 2024

42168360R10043